FIRST 50 LEFT-HAND PATTERNS

YOU SHOULD PLAY ON PIANO

by Alistair Watson

ISBN 979-8-3501-5313-2

Scan. Practice. Play.

HAL•LEONARD®
A Muse Group Company

Visit Hal Leonard Online at
www.halleonard.com

World headquarters, contact:
Hal Leonard
Email: info@halleonard.com

In Europe, contact:
Hal Leonard Europe Limited
Email: info@halleonardeurope.com

In Australia, contact:
Hal Leonard Australia Pty. Ltd.
Email: info@halleonard.com.au

INTRODUCTION

Welcome to *First 50 Left-Hand Patterns You Should Play on Piano.* Throughout this book, you will find some of the most popular and commonly used patterns for the left hand. You will need to be able to read a little music for this book and there are piano keyboard diagrams showing you where the principal notes are. You'll also notice numbers on the music and diagrams, suggesting possible fingering you could use. Each left-hand pattern is presented in its basic form, followed by an extract of music. You'll love being able to celebrate your skills straight away, developing your left hand and playing great music at the same time!

To play the piano safely and comfortably, make sure that you observe the following.

Sitting at the Piano

- Sit tall and lean slightly forward, balancing your body weight on the front half of the piano bench.
- Keep your feet flat on the floor.
- Adjust the bench height so that your forearm is parallel to the floor and your fingertips are touching the surface of the keys.

Hand Position

Let your arms hang relaxed at your sides. Notice how your hands stay gently curved. Keep your hands relaxed and curved as you raise them to the piano keyboard. When you are playing the piano, keep your fingers in this relaxed, curved position.

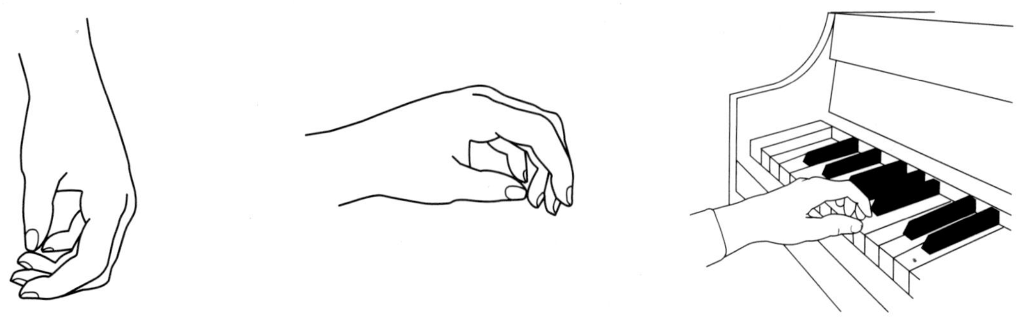

CONTENTS

PATTERN 1

WHOLE NOTES

Pattern Tip: This is the simplest pattern you can play with the left hand. Whole notes, each lasting a full measure, sit underneath your right-hand melody line. Each note just provides an outline of the harmony, giving the bare bones of support for your right hand. This pattern can be a gateway to playing easy arrangements of many popular hits, forming the underlying accompaniment to a range of music from Queen to Sam Smith!

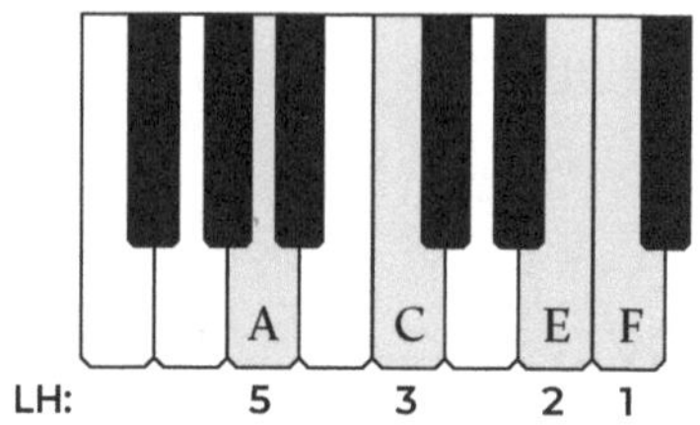

Basic Progression

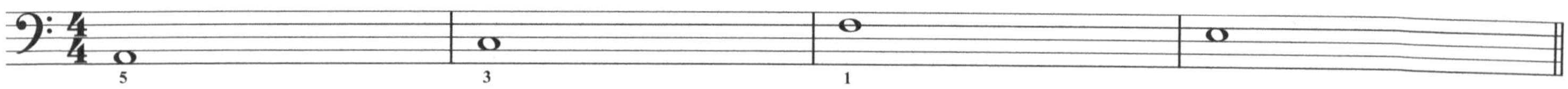

Performance Style

PATTERN 2

QUARTER NOTES

Pattern Tip: A straightforward and common pattern, notes are played on every beat by the left hand. This gives a sense of forward momentum, with each beat present underneath the texture. You can find applications of this type of pattern in many different musical styles including classical music, as heard in Handel's *The Arrival of the Queen of Sheba*.

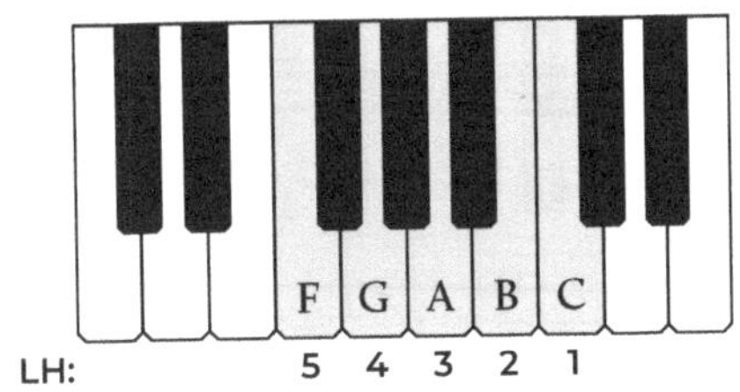

Basic Progression

Performance Style

PATTERN 3

BARE FIFTH

Pattern Tip: This is one of the simplest patterns for the left hand. Here, you play two notes a fifth apart. This **bare fifth** is a "building block" pattern that is useful for playing songs in different musical styles, particularly rock music by bands like Oasis. You just need a strong thumb and pinky finger, and to be able to count to four!

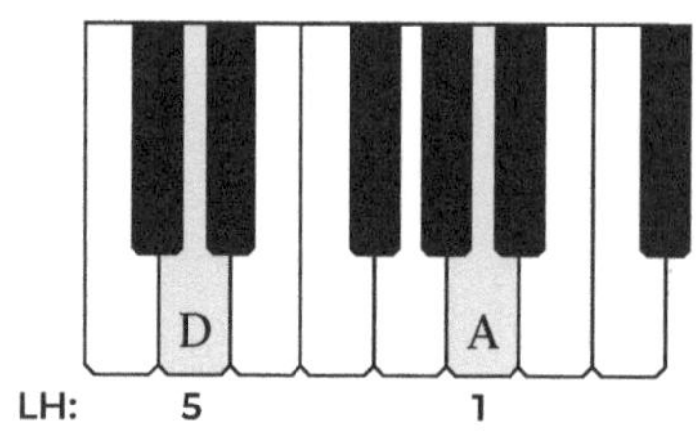

Basic Pattern

Performance Style

PATTERN 4

BARE FIFTH EXTENSION

Pattern Tip: This pattern simply extends the bare fifth. In a measure of 4/4, you play two half notes with your thumb over a whole note in the bass. The additional top note adds interest and helps drive the music forward. It's a staple element of many pop and rock songs, including in music of The Beatles.

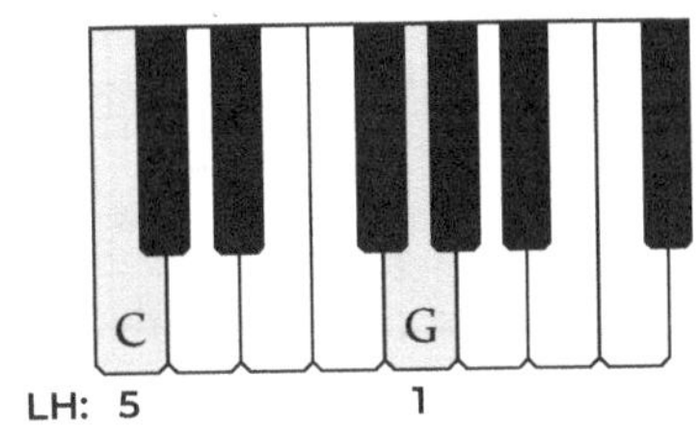

Basic Pattern

Performance Style

PATTERN 5

BARE FIFTH WITH BASS PULSE

Pattern Tip: Here, we extend the bare fifth by adding quarter notes in the bass. Your pinky finger becomes the cornerstone and must play firmly on each beat. Move your whole hand up and down as a block. This device is great for imitating the style of alternative rock bands like Nirvana. If you're playing rock, play it loud!

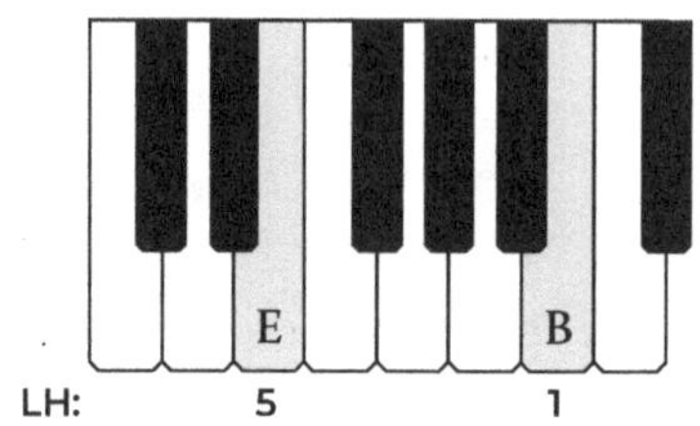

Basic Pattern

Performance Style

PATTERN 6

BASIC TRIAD

Pattern Tip: This is a straightforward pattern applying a new concept. The **triad** is a chord of three notes and you can play it with fingers 5–3–1. Once you've mastered the set shape try to move your hand as a solid block, with the notes sounding perfectly together. Because the chord doesn't involve movement, it gives your right hand space to play the melody. In its most basic form, this pattern can be found in lots of simple traditional music, including Christmas carols such as "We Wish You a Merry Christmas."

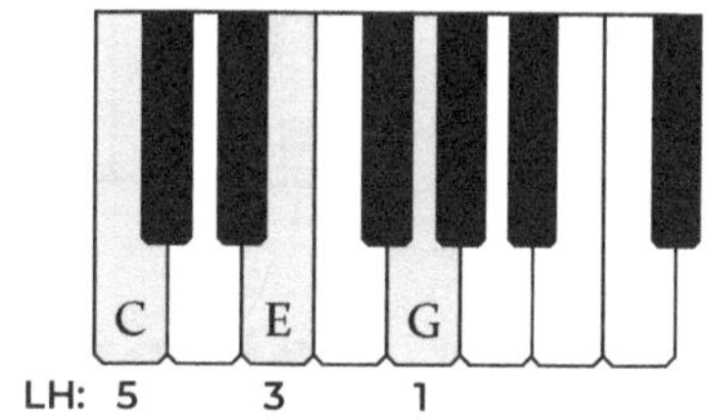

Basic Pattern

Performance Style

PATTERN 7

BLOCK CHORD WITH MOVEMENT

Pattern Tip: This is a fundamental pattern to many musical styles, where the left hand continually plays a full triad. Move in quarter notes with a chord on each beat of the measure, taking care to get all three notes down together each time. This creates what we call **block chord** movement. The pattern is the foundation for playing simple arrangements of most popular music, from *Sesame Street* to *KPop Demon Hunters*!

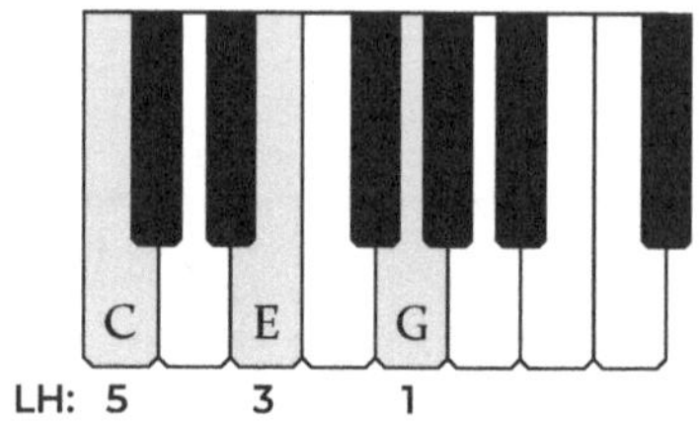

Basic Pattern

Performance Style

PATTERN 8

SCALE

Pattern Tip: The humble **scale** is an essential pattern to come to grips with when learning the piano. It is super useful in so many contexts and, as a left-hand pattern, found in all types of classical and popular artists, from Mozart to David Bowie! Use next-door fingers for next-door notes and try to move over and under the thumb with the correct finger.

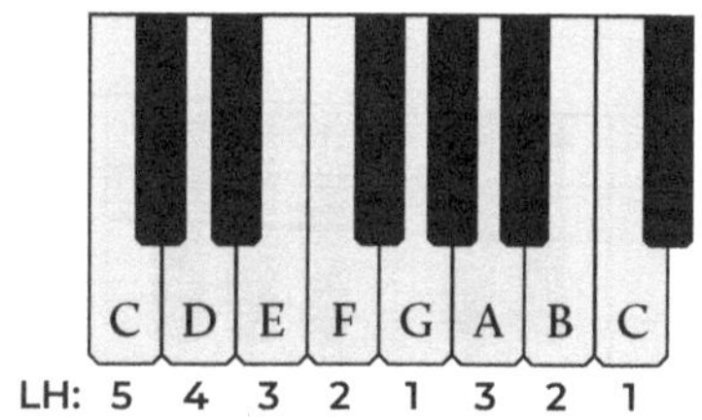

Basic Pattern

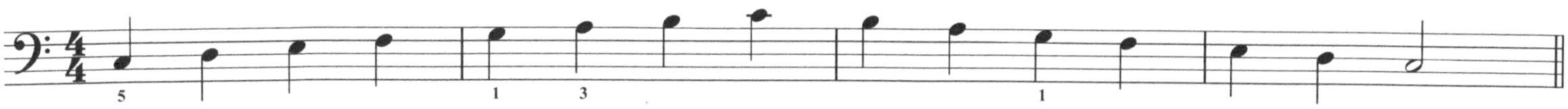

Performance Style

PATTERN 9

DESCENDING BASS

Pattern Tip: An absolute staple in music across genres, from Beethoven to Ray Charles and Billy Joel, this pattern carries a more clearly defined melodic shape than most. It is a **descending** line (getting lower in pitch) that makes use of the lowered seventh and sixth degrees of the scale, usually implying a minor key.

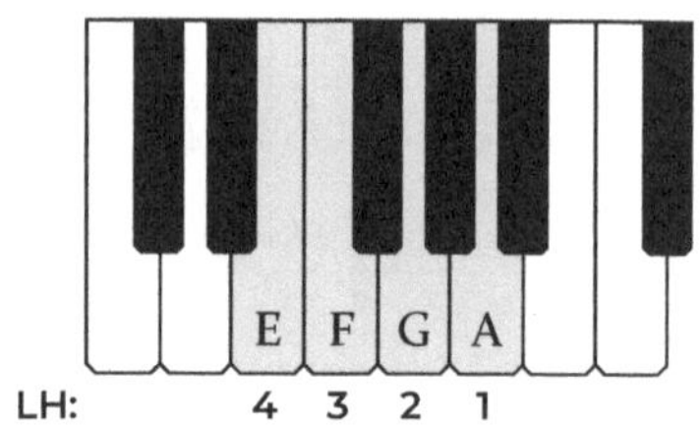

Basic Pattern

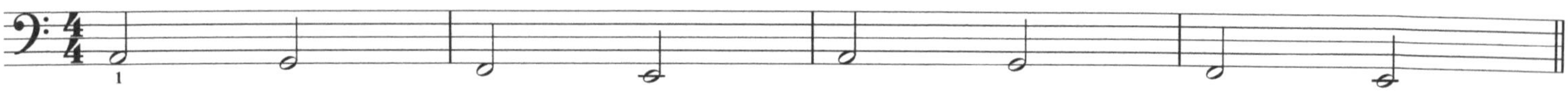

Performance Style

PATTERN 10

DOTTED RHYTHM

Pattern Tip: Dotted rhythms are very common in accompanying patterns for all musical styles. A dot by a notehead extends its duration by half. In these patterns, the dotted note is usually followed by one of shorter value, adding a little rhythmic interest into the accompaniment. Here, a pattern reminiscent of Beethoven's famous "Ode to Joy" stays on one note throughout each measure, giving you time to look ahead to what's coming up.

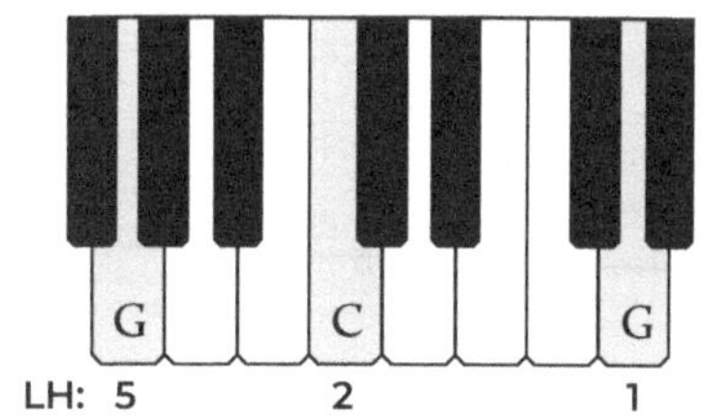

Basic Pattern

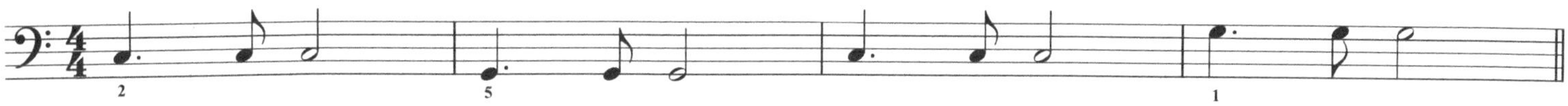

Performance Style

PATTERN 11

DOTTED BLOCK CHORD

Pattern Tip: This pattern expands upon the dotted rhythm in a way common to many popular songwriters like John Legend. The first chord is extended and a **tie** joins the second chord to the third, so that there is an **off-beat** feel. You need a strong sense of pulse, here.

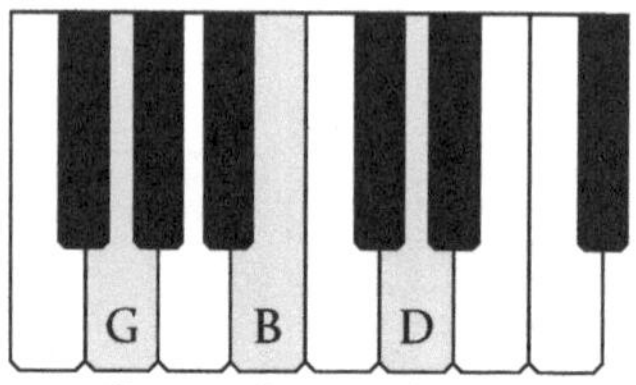

LH: 5 3 1

Basic Pattern

Performance Style

PATTERN 12

BARE FIFTH IN EIGHTH NOTES

Pattern Tip: Exploited in the songwriting of artists as diverse as Adele and Green Day, the left hand breaks down our previous bare fifth pattern into repeated eighth notes. This gives the effect of a heavy beat, which really drives the music along.

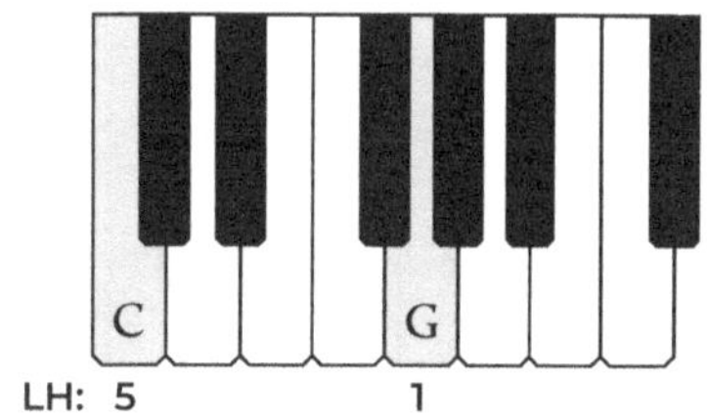

Basic Pattern

Performance Style

PATTERN 13

BROKEN CHORD

Pattern Tip: This is a common pattern, where a chord is simply broken down into its constituent notes. Take a triad and play each note individually from bottom to top in a continuous, rolling manner. Such patterns are often found in slow, peaceful music such as the Christmas evergreen "O Holy Night."

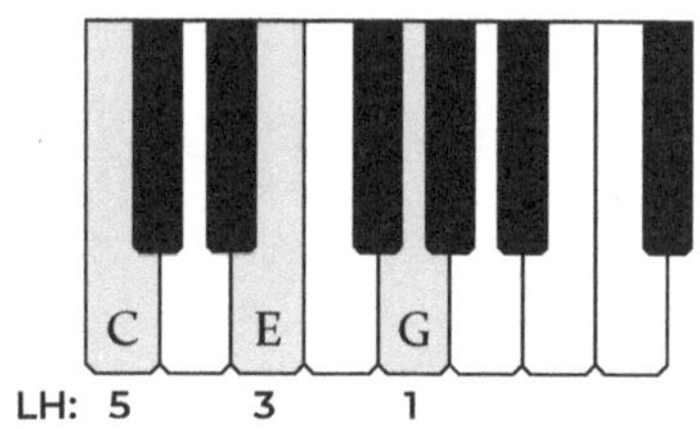

Basic Pattern

Performance Style

PATTERN 14

ARPEGGIO SHELL

Pattern Tip: Often found in traditional folk songs like "Scarborough Fair," this pattern outlines an **arpeggio**, with the fifth anchoring in the middle. You need to spread your hand over an octave, although being able to reach this isn't essential. Arm movement can help to guide your fingers, here.

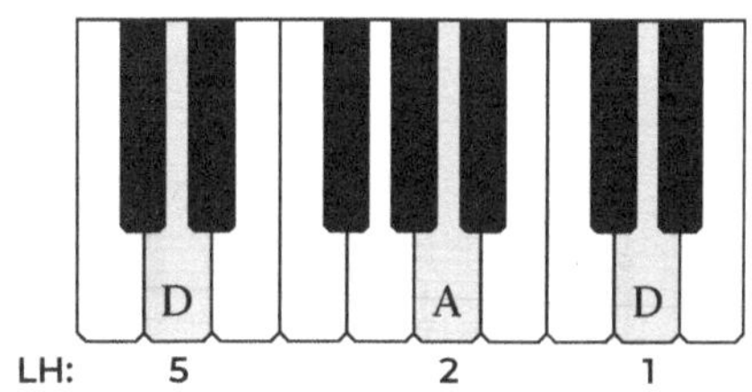

Basic Pattern

Performance Style

PATTERN 15

ARPEGGIO

Pattern Tip: One of the most frequently used left-hand patterns, this is found in music from practically every era and style. Building on the arpeggio shell, the full arpeggio just fills in the gaps, adding the third. You can choose which finger to put on the second note: either finger number 3 or 4. Your choice may well depend on where you are on the keyboard. Often exploited as a device for more pensive songwriting, this is a pattern found in reflective numbers such as in the music of Leonard Cohen.

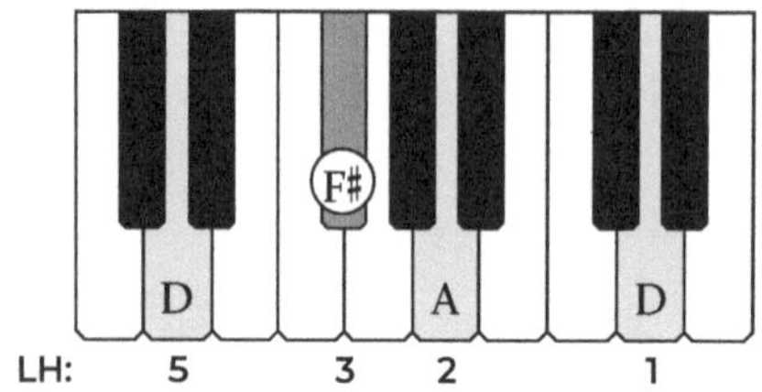

Basic Pattern

Performance Style

PATTERN 16

ARPEGGIO VARIATION

Pattern Tip: If you listen to Handel's popular *Zadok the Priest*, you'll hear this pattern in action. Simply a different version of the arpeggio, our left hand plays all four notes **ascending** (going up in pitch) before jumping back to the bottom note. This gives a sense of urgency, driving the music forward.

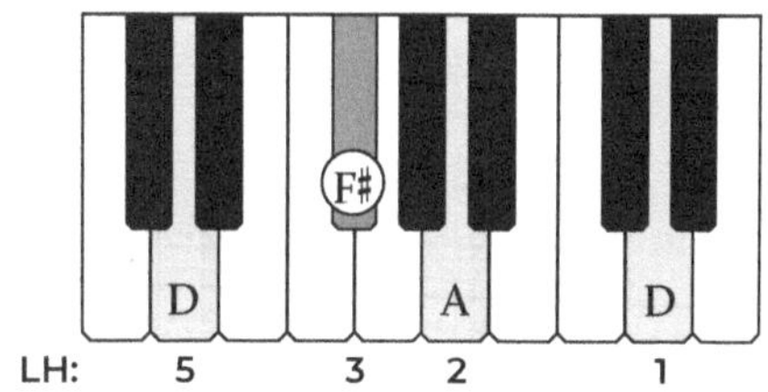

Basic Pattern

Performance Style

PATTERN 17

ALBERTI BASS

Pattern Tip: Put your hand in the standard triad position, between C and G. Then, play a broken-chord pattern in the pitch order "low–high–middle–high." Here, the middle note sounds third in each group. You can then transfer this pattern to different broken-chord shapes. Named after the eighteenth-century composer Domenico Alberti, the pattern became particularly common in music of the Classical era, such as Mozart's Piano Sonata No. 16, K 545.

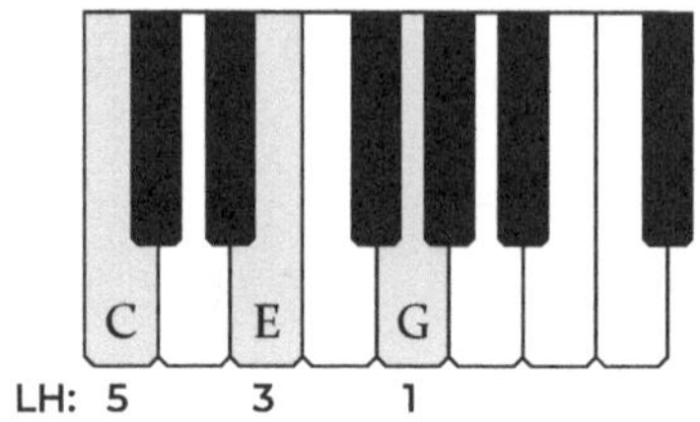

Basic Pattern

Performance Style

PATTERN 18

ARPGEGGIO WITH HELD BASS

Pattern Tip: This pattern is often found in songs with a 3/4 or 6/8 time signature, such as "The House of the Rising Sun." It involves a held bass note followed by the remaining arpeggio. This bass note underpins the harmony: use of the pedal may help.

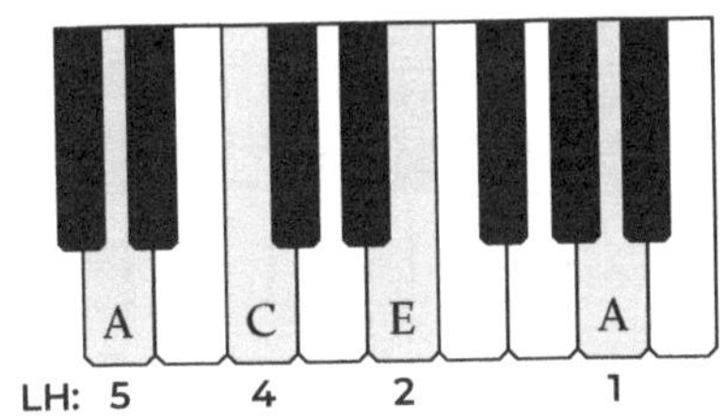

Basic Pattern

Performance Style

PATTERN 19

BOUNCY QUARTER NOTES

Pattern Tip: A fun and quite straightforward pattern, repeated quarter notes, played in a spiky (**staccato**) manner, alternate over a fifth. The use of this interval gives an outline of harmony and the bouncy articulation can be either playful or foreboding, as in the slightly ominous "In the Hall of the Mountain King" by Grieg.

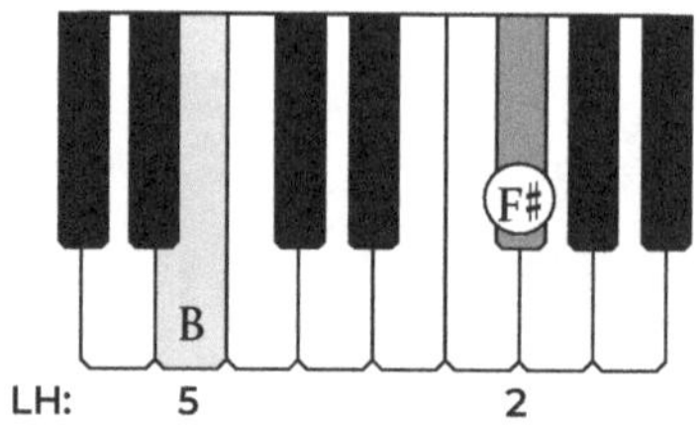

Basic Pattern

Performance Style

PATTERN 20

WALTZ

Pattern Tip: Some of the most famous waltzes in music were written by the nineteenth-century, Austrian composer Johann Strauss II. His *The Blue Danube* waltz is found everywhere, from concert halls to television commercials! The waltz is a dance, often with three beats in a measure. Its left-hand pattern involves a bass note followed by two chords. This creates a strong downbeat, with harmony on beats 2 and 3.

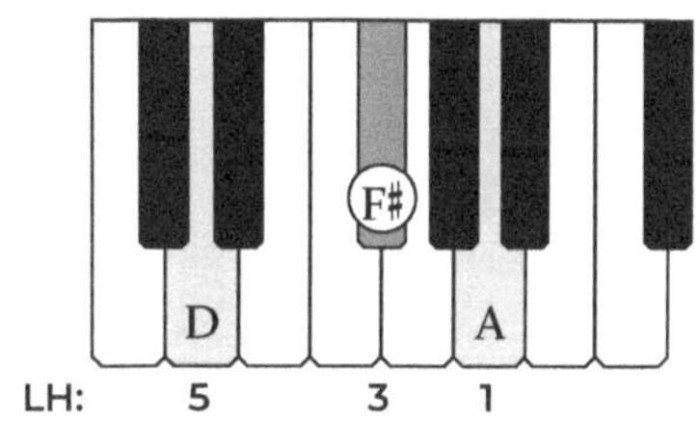

Basic Pattern

Performance Style

PATTERN 21

WALTZ VARIATION

Pattern Tip: Some famous classical waltzes, such as Tchaikovsky's waltz from *Sleeping Beauty*, vary our standard accompaniment pattern. Here, the bass note changes between the root and the fifth. This adds harmonic variety and textural interest.

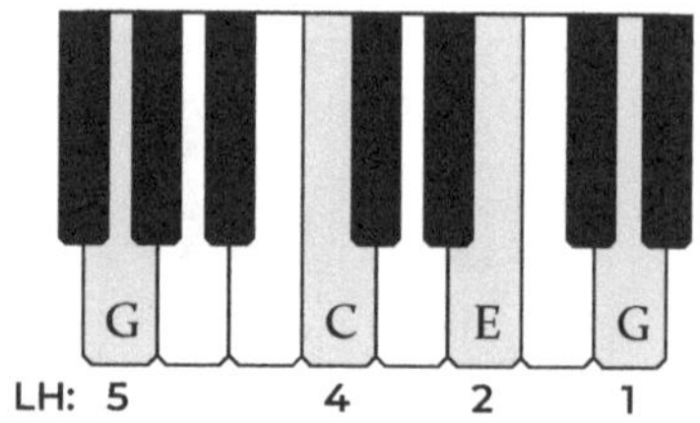

Basic Pattern

Performance Style

PATTERN 22

ADVANCED WALTZ

Pattern Tip: Reminiscent of famous opera songs (**arias**) by Giuseppe Verdi such as "La donna è mobile," this more challenging pattern involved notes on beats 2 and 3 that are further away! Stretch out your hand so that you can reach up to the tenth (beyond the octave). You can use either finger 3 or 2 on the middle note.

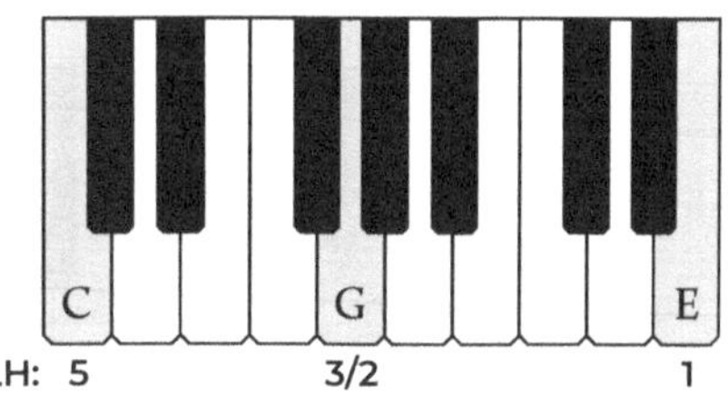

Basic Pattern

Performance Style

PATTERN 23

BOOM-CHUCK

Pattern Tip: Often used to accompany simple tunes like "Twinkle, Twinkle Little Star," this left-hand pattern breaks the triad down into a bass-chord format, using repeated fingering. It's especially useful for injecting a little more interest into the accompaniment beyond merely playing solid, block chords. Learning this pattern can be aided by invoking a gentle rocking motion in your wrist.

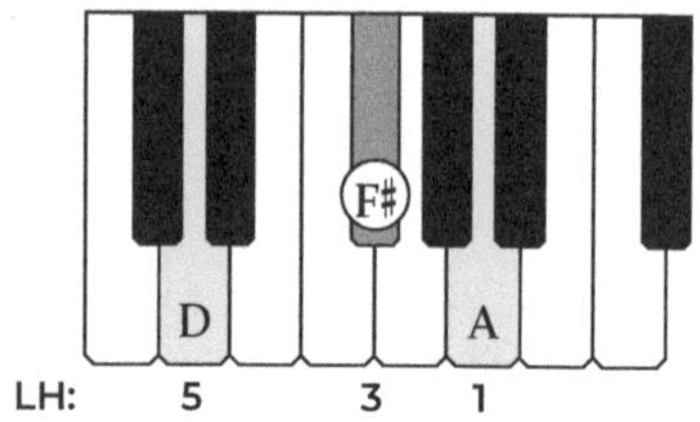

Basic Pattern

Performance Style

PATTERN 24

ARPEGGIO TO THE TENTH

Pattern Tip: Gentle music such as the contemporary piano works of Richard Clayderman often uses a pattern that extends the arpeggio beyond an octave spread. Don't worry if you can't reach; your arm movement will help, coaxing the elbow from side to side. Here, the fifth acts as a pivot between the top and bottom notes. You can use either finger number 2 or 3, a choice that may depend on where you are on the keyboard. This pattern produces a feeling of space, lending a warm bed of harmony underneath your melody line.

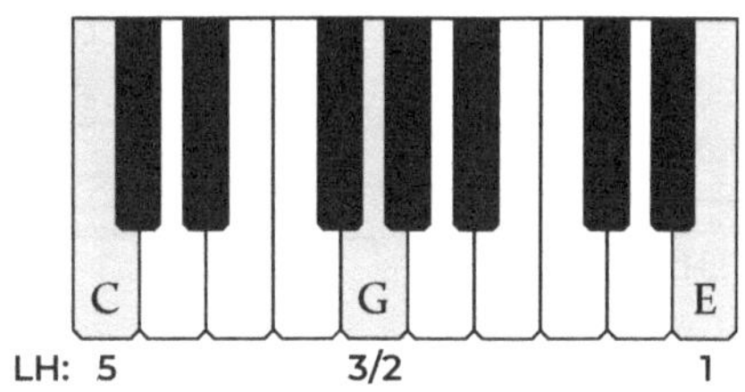

Basic Pattern

Performance Style

PATTERN 25

ROLLING EIGHTHS

Pattern Tip: Common to contemporary classical piano styles such as the works of Ludovico Einaudi, this is a good pattern for instilling movement in your accompaniments. Move your left hand up and down the keyboard as a solid block, playing the root, fifth, and upper octave of each chord in rolling eighths. The pattern keeps returning to the fifth, which acts as a pivot.

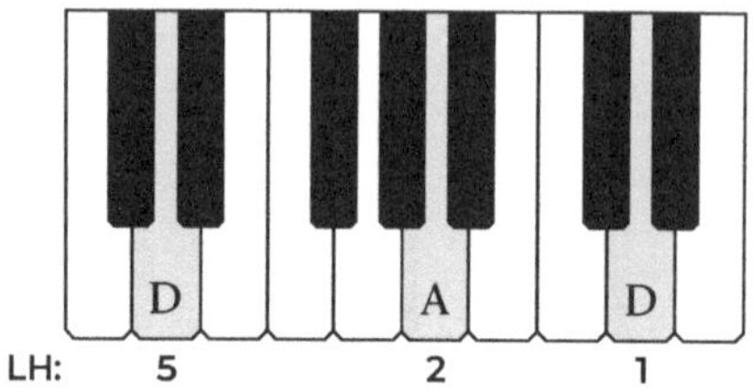

Basic Pattern

Performance Style

PATTERN 26

ROLLING TO THE TENTH

Pattern Tip: This "peaceful piano" pattern extends our left-hand rolling eighths beyond the octave, up to the tenth. You can choose which finger to put on the middle note: either 2 or 3. As is so often the case, this decision may be dependent upon where you are on the keyboard.

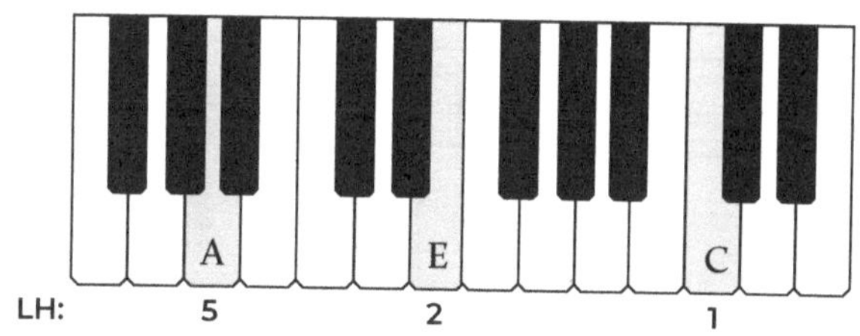

Basic Pattern

Performance Style

PATTERN 27

BASS AND TEXTURE

Pattern Tip: This more advanced pattern requires you to hold a bass note with the pinky finger, while playing alternating eighth notes above. Found in contemporary piano styles such as those of Einaudi and Yann Tiersen, eighth notes enrich the texture by filling out the harmony. A simple right hand might play single melody notes above.

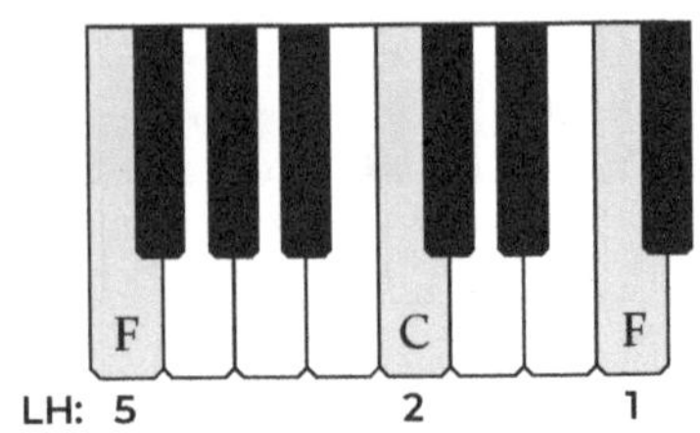

Basic Pattern

Performance Style

PATTERN 28

DOTTED BASS AND TEXTURE

Pattern Tip: This much used left-hand technique extends that of Pattern 27, featuring eighth-note movement above a held, dotted bass. Move your hand up and down as a block, always using the same fingering.

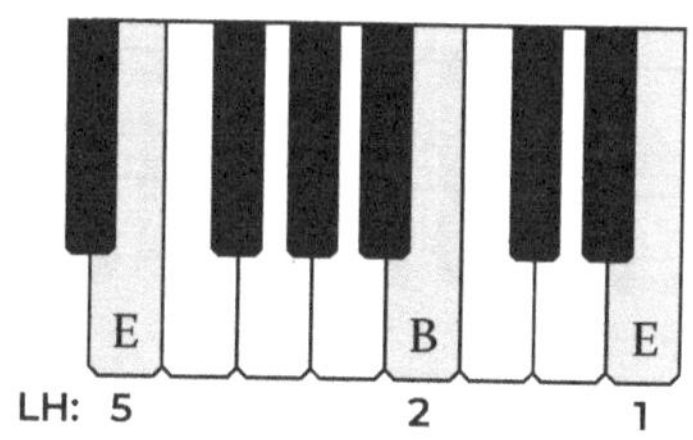

Basic Pattern

Performance Style

PATTERN 29

EXTENDED MOVING EIGHTHS

Pattern Tip: Hitherto a common left-hand pattern in many genres of piano music, this accompaniment style has been made especially recognizable by more modern contemporary classical writing. It's especially good for maintaining a sense of movement in your left hand. Here, you do need to be able to reach a full octave. If this isn't possible, you could always miss out the top note. Again, the fifth acts as a pivot between the octave and the sixth.

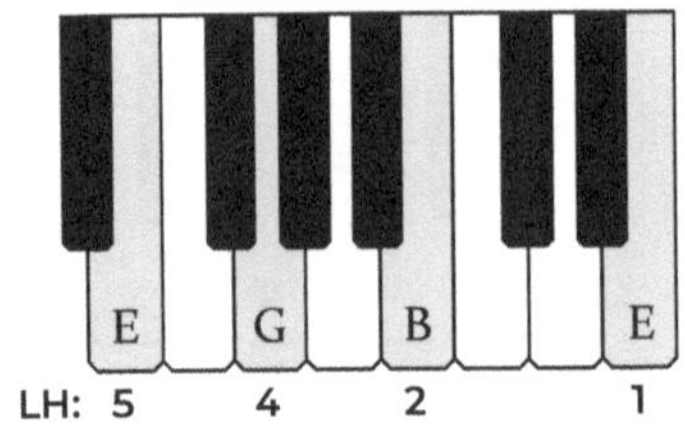

Basic Pattern

Performance Style

PATTERN 30

ROCK & POP BASS-CHORD

Pattern Tip: Common in many popular and rock songs such as music by The Beatles, this pattern has the left hand playing a bass note followed by an upper chord. Try to hold the half note, which will provide a fuller sense of harmony. This is particularly effective when moving downwards in step.

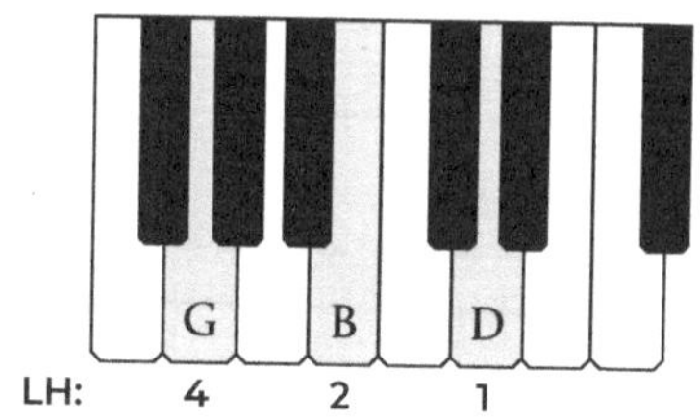

Basic Pattern

Performance Style

PATTERN 31

BASS-CHORD IN THREE

Pattern Tip: As exemplified in Erik Satie's timeless *Gymnopédie No. 1,* this pattern has the left hand applying our bass-chord pattern in triple time. As a result, the chord has longer to ring before the next bass note. Using the pedal for the examples below will be essential, due to the chord notes being much higher up the keyboard.

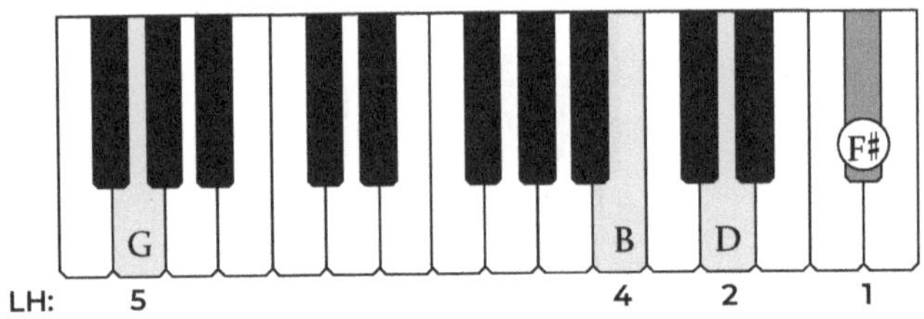

Basic Pattern

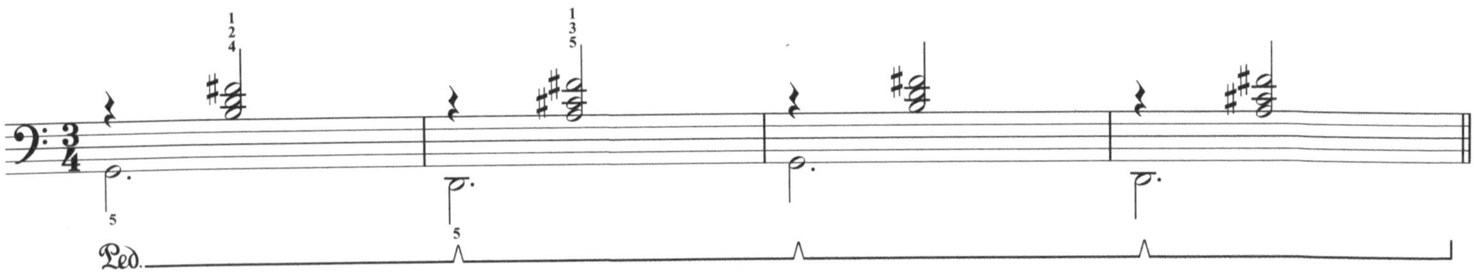

Performance Style

PATTERN 32

ROCK OCTAVES

Pattern Tip: Playing a full octave is a great way of increasing the presence of the bass in your left-hand patterns. Octaves sound good underneath chords, giving extra weight and support. Once you're comfortable playing octaves, you can add them into virtually any popular song.

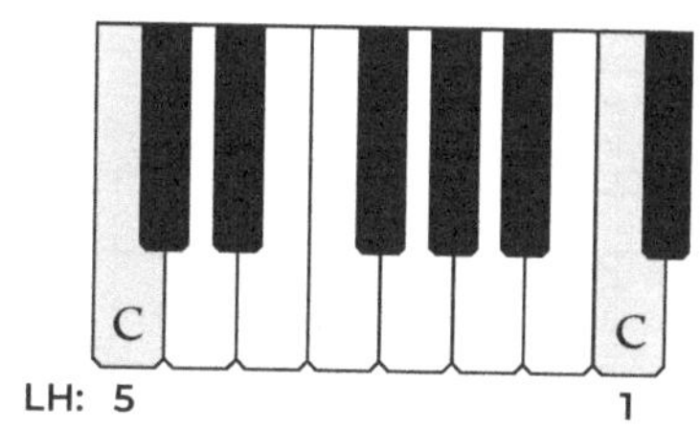

Basic Pattern

Performance Style

PATTERN 33

ROCKING OCTAVES

Pattern Tip: Popular songs by bands like ABBA and Derek and the Dominos demonstrate how drama and momentum can be created through a left-hand accompaniment. For this pattern, you need to be able to reach a full octave, as you're constantly moving up and down. Real depth and dynamism can be added to the music, as a result.

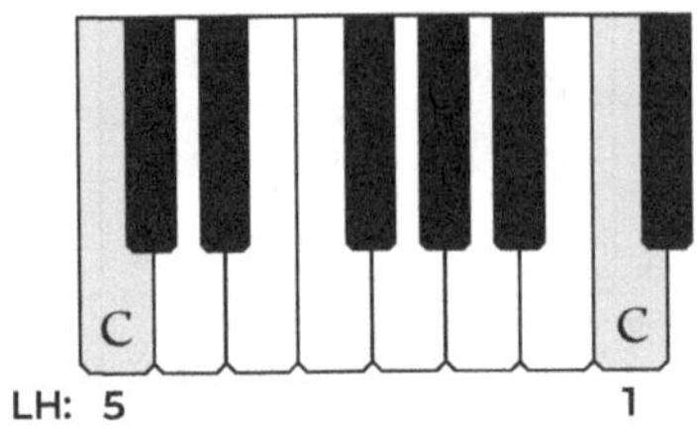

Basic Pattern

Performance Style

PATTERN 34

WALKING BASS

Pattern Tip: This is a very common pattern, where your left hand plays a crucial role in injecting movement and interest into your playing. It can be found in countless evergreen hits such as the songs of Bart Howard. The left hand provides the harmonic bass but is constantly moving ("walking") towards the next chord. This is usually played with quarter notes but be alive to the occasional "skip" where an eighth note is added.

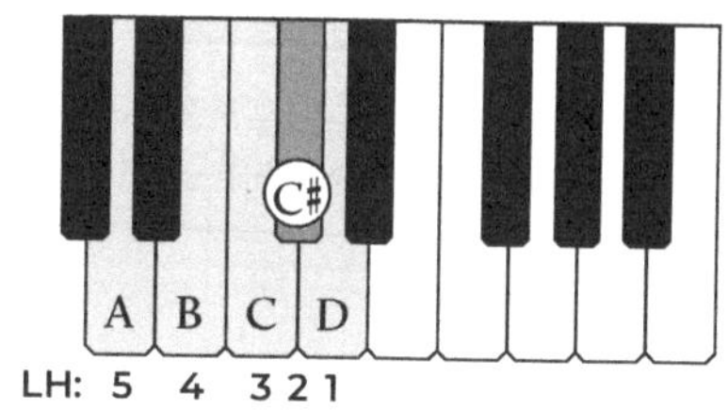

Basic Pattern

Performance Style

PATTERN 35

WALKING TO THE SEVENTH

Pattern Tip: This is a variation on the walking bass line we encountered in the previous pattern. Its unique sound is derived from the fact that it specifically moves up to the seventh and back again, giving a bluesy sonority. It is often used in the "12-bar blues" form and is reminiscent of music by artists like Elvis Presley and Bill Haley & His Comets.

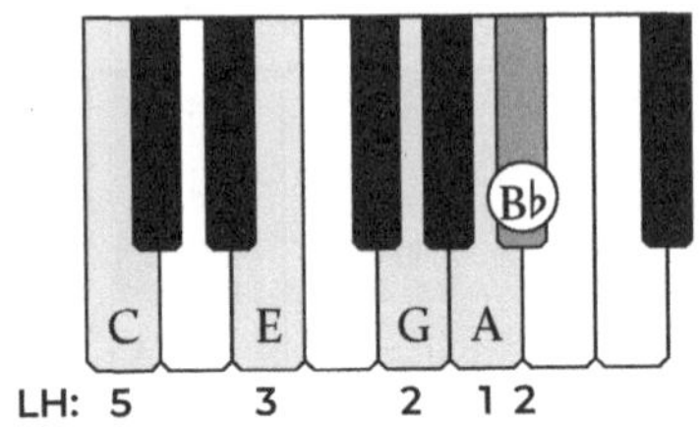

Basic Pattern

Performance Style

PATTERN 36

BLUES SWING

Pattern Tip: This is a very common blues pattern. Spread your left hand beyond the five-finger position by one note, so that you can reach the sixth. (Here, note A). Play with a rocking motion, using eighth notes **swung** in pairs; a languid, "long-short" rhythm that will give the music a chilled character.

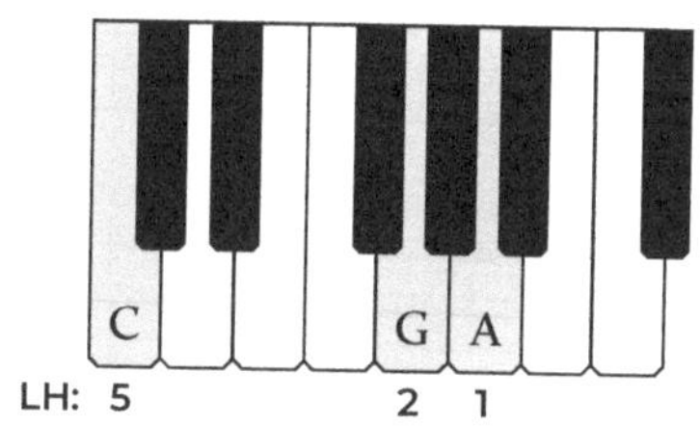

Basic Pattern

Performance Style

PATTERN 37

BLUES BOOGIE

Pattern Tip: The driving style of boogie songwriters like Otha Hayes provides a great example of this energetic pattern, which uses fast-moving eighth notes. In each measure, the pattern repeats the root before moving up to the sixth. Try it in different keys and across varied harmonic progressions. Here, eighth notes are played straight as written.

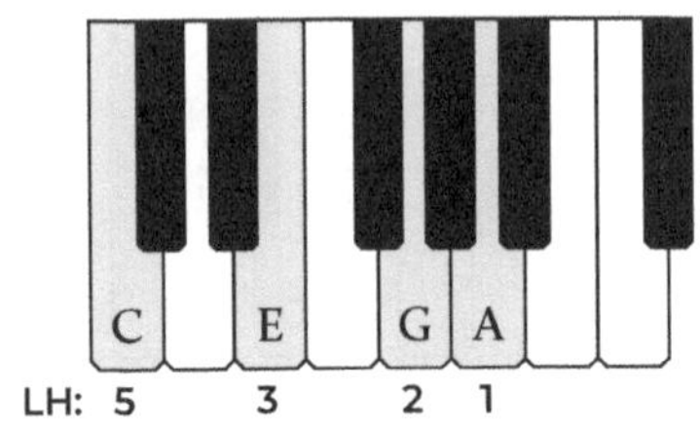

Basic Pattern

Performance Style

PATTERN 38

STRIDE

Pattern Tip: Stride piano is a very common left-hand technique, made famous by "ragtime" jazz pianists and heard in works such as *The Entertainer* by Scott Joplin. The pattern is characterized by a bass note followed by a higher chord. This induces the left hand to "stride" across the keyboard. In any measure of 4/4, the lowest bass note will typically land on beats 1 and 3, and the chords on beats 2 and 4.

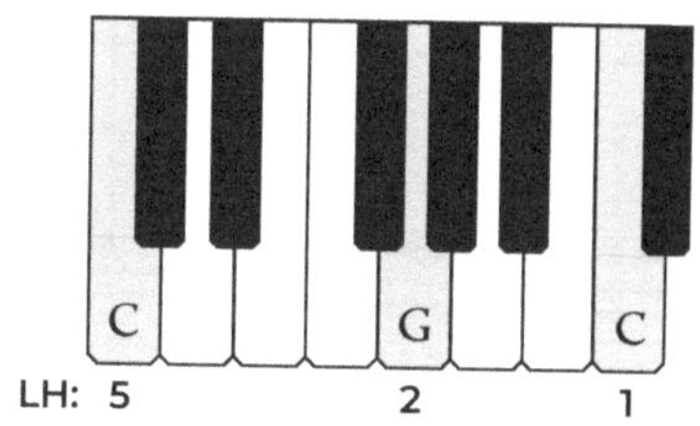

Basic Pattern

Performance Style

PATTERN 39

BLUES SHUFFLE

Pattern Tip: This classic blues pattern is found across many popular genres and artists, from Buddy Holly to Eric Clapton. Here, you begin playing the fifth but extend upwards to the sixth and seventh. Deliberately dotted rhythms give the left hand a sense of drive.

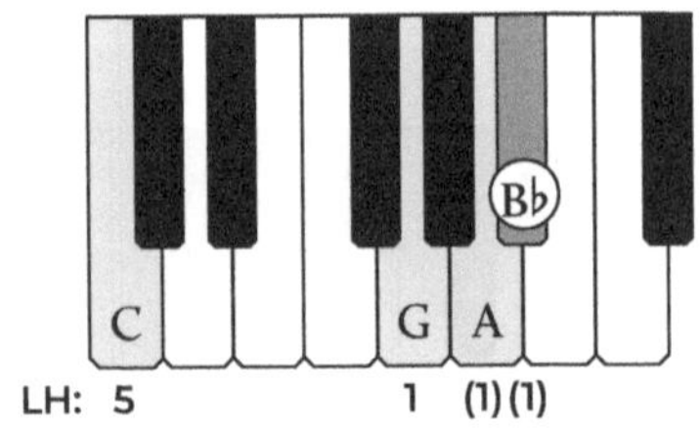

Basic Pattern

Performance Style

PATTERN 40

STRAIGHT BOOGIE

Pattern Tip: Another classic blues pattern that has been exploited by numerous popular artists such as Led Zeppelin. This time with straight eighths, the left hand begins with a bare fifth before progressing through various scale degrees. It has a real "chugging" feel.

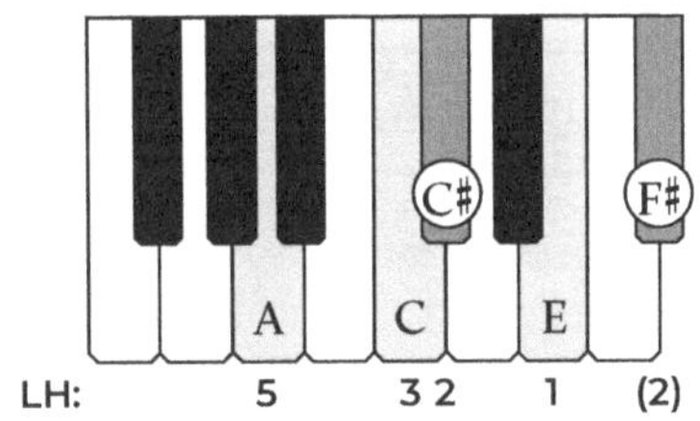

Basic Pattern

Performance Style

PATTERN 41

BARRELHOUSE

Pattern Tip: Working particularly well with a swung melody, this pattern states a bare fifth before alternating with the sixth. Here, the lowest bass stays the same throughout but the top note keeps changing. Perfect for dancing and rowdy audiences, the style gets its name from the makeshift saloons of the American south where it thrived, and where the liquor was served straight out of barrels.

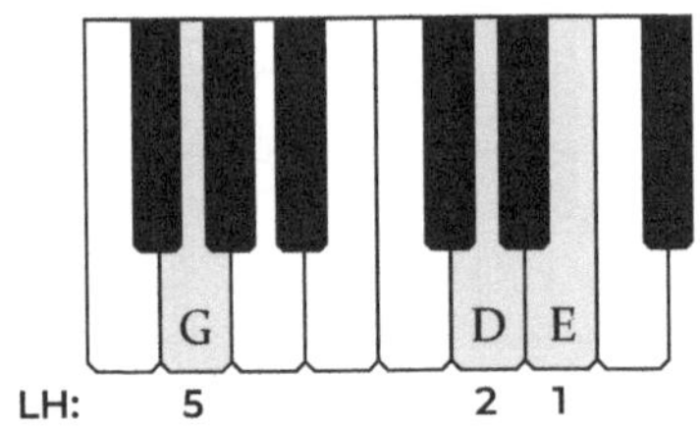

Basic Pattern

Performance Style

PATTERN 42

SEVENTH CHORD

Pattern Tip: In this pattern the left hand plays a **seventh chord**, (the root and the seventh note together with either the third or the fifth sitting in the middle). It is a useful building block, as seventh chords are common to most styles of music. Music of the "Great American Songbook," such as the works of Irving Berlin, George Gershwin, and Harold Arlen, is positively bursting with these chords.

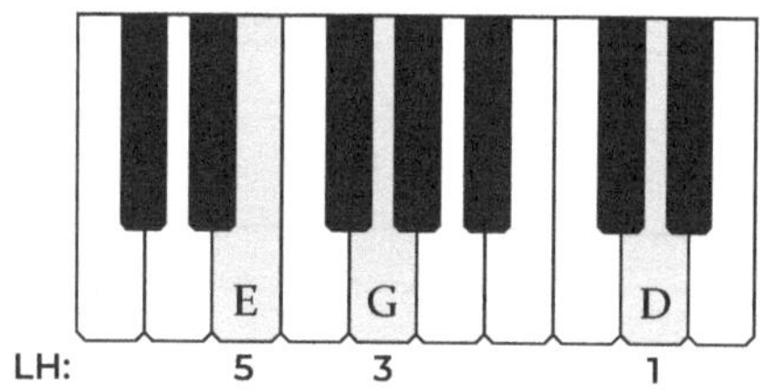

Basic Pattern

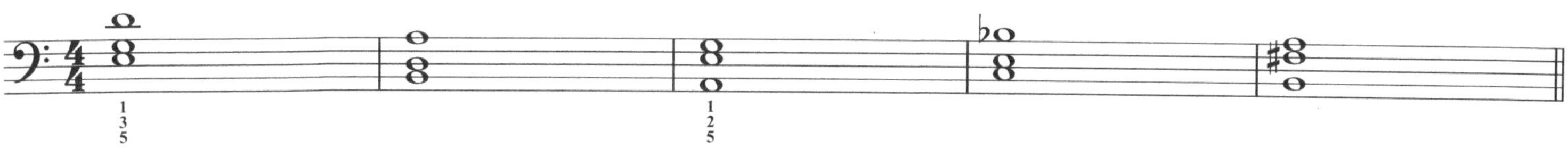

Performance Style

PATTERN 43

SEVENTH SHELL

Pattern Tip: This pattern utilizes the seventh but without the third in the middle, hence its "shell" voicing. It lends a particular identity to genres like soul and R&B, as seen in the songs of Marvin Gaye. An easier stretch than the octave, the seventh interval between pinky and thumb can be the full focus here, without notes in the middle to worry about.

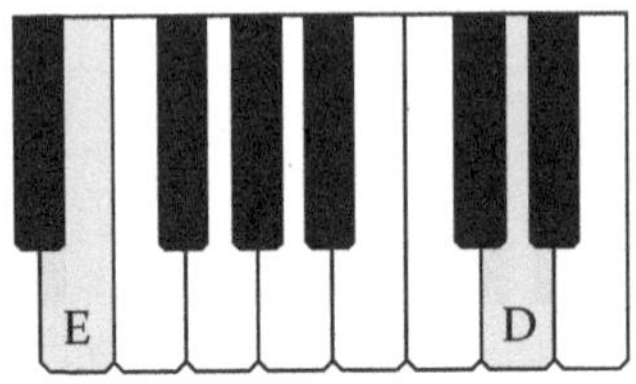

LH: 5 1

Basic Pattern

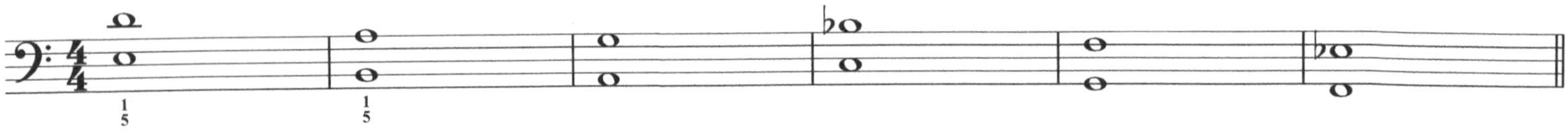

Performance Style

PATTERN 44

BLUES WALKING BASS

Pattern Tip: This driving left-hand pattern gives a particular flavor to our learned walking bass, using both the minor and major third, and the sixth. Here, the left hand has constantly moving eighth notes. Again, feel free to experiment by moving through different harmonic progressions.

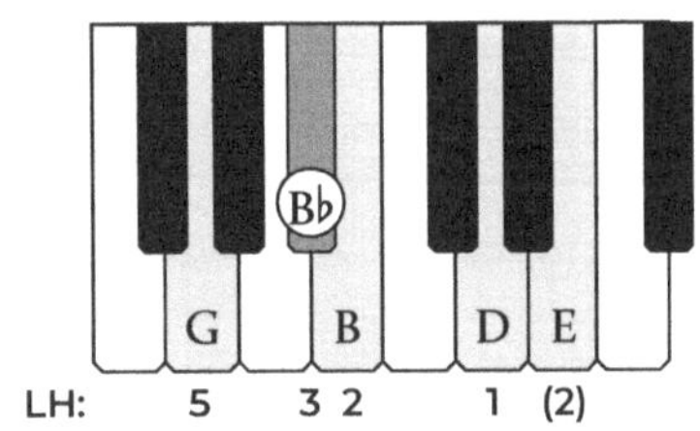

Basic Pattern

Performance Style

PATTERN 45

MAMBO

Pattern Tip: This is a more advanced left-hand groove involving a tricky rhythmic pattern that is spread over two measures. Note the syncopation at the end of the first measure, characteristic of famous popular songs in this genre.

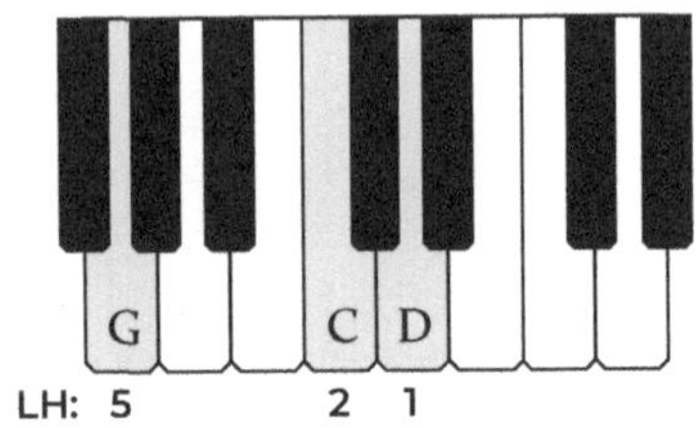

Basic Pattern

Performance Style

PATTERN 46

DOTTED LATIN

Pattern Tip: A characteristic dotted rhythm gives character and rhythmic drive to many Latin popular songs. The left hand will need to cover an octave, although if you can't reach this the rolling nature of the figure means your arm movement may help.

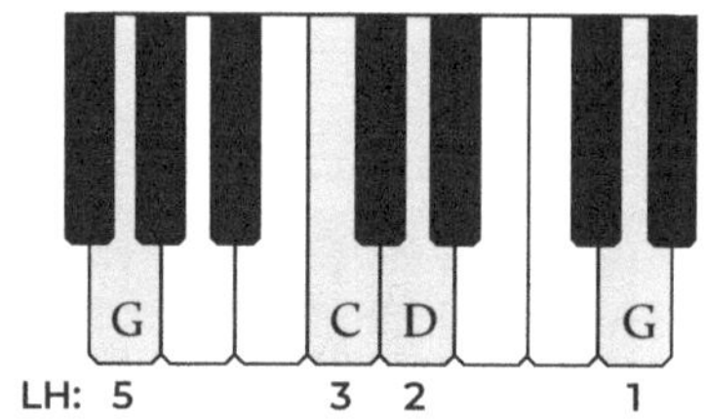

Basic Pattern

Performance Style

PATTERN 47

MONTUNO

Pattern Tip: This is a very advanced salsa pattern that repeats over two measures. It is highly **syncopated** (off-beat), with only the first and second notes landing on the beat. It is also harmonically interesting, making use of the raised seventh juxtaposed against the natural sixth. You can imagine a firm drumbeat underpinning this pattern. Its name has roots in the styles of Cuban "son" music, and the pattern has been exploited across numerous genres from Broadway to Disney!

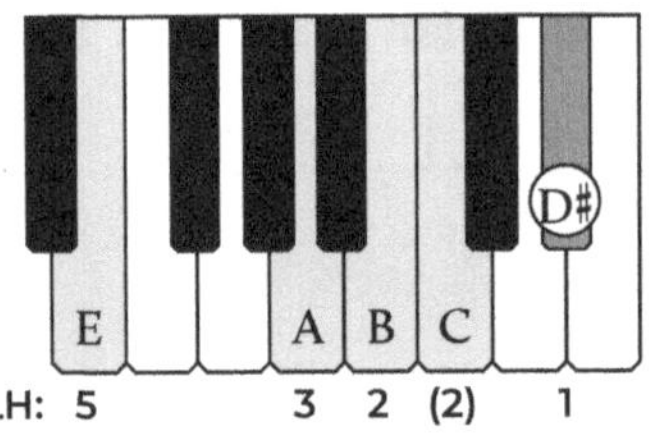

Basic Pattern

Performance Style

PATTERN 48

DOTTED NEAPOLITAN

Pattern Tip: Exploited in famous classical songs such as *O sole mio*, this is another pattern characterized by a dotted rhythm. The left hand propels the music forward. It is a combination of two patterns encountered earlier in the book: "Dotted Rhythm" and "Arpeggio Shell."

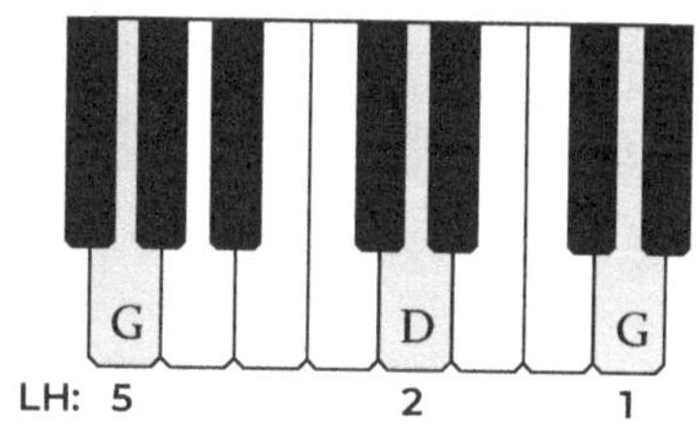

Basic Pattern

Performance Style

PATTERN 49

BOOGIE OCTAVES

Pattern Tip: This is a more advanced pattern. You need to be comfortable playing octaves, moving up and down the keyboard. The pattern alternates between lower and upper octaves, moving up to the seventh in a manner typical of the boogie style.

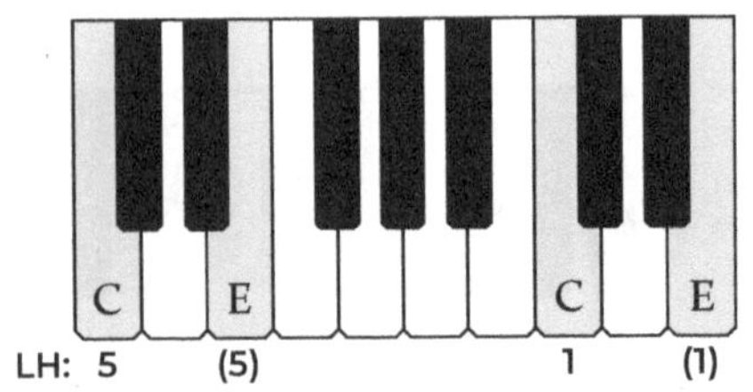

Basic Pattern

Performance Style

PATTERN 50

MOTOWN OCTAVES

Pattern Tip: In this pattern, the left hand plays a full octave juxtaposed against eighth notes. The characteristic push in the middle of the measure became a calling card of Motown greats such as Holland-Dozier-Holland and The Temptations.

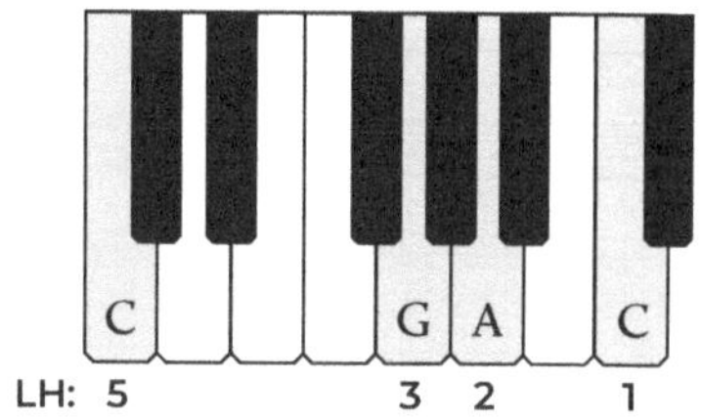

Basic Pattern

Performance Style

0225
393